STEVEN APPLEBY was born in Northumberland in the 1950's, and spent most of his childhood in Yorkshire. He studied graphic design at Newcastle-upon-Tyne Polytechnic and illustration at the Royal College of Art. He enjoys raucous popular music and dressing fashionably.
Sometimes he has been allowed to design posters for other people and contribute drawings to magazines.
His devotion to his kitten and parrot was rewarded by their untimely demise. He would like to own animals that do not die.

GEORGE MOULE was born in London in 1954, after which his family moved to Australia. He studied Modern Languages at Edinburgh University. He has worked as a plasterer, salesman, painter, carpenter, barman, costume maker, agent, etcetera, and once had a job which allowed him to do a bit of cooking. He has contributed to a number of magazines on museums, cookery, travel and items of historical interest. He contracted various diseases in 1975 but survived and he now works for a British film company in Los Angeles.

This book is their first.

"No, honestly, it was simply delicious
but I couldn't eat another mouthful."

A Kitchen Complement
by
George Moule & Steven Appleby

Pan Books
London & Sydney

To our Mothers.

First published 1984 by Pan Books Ltd,
Cavaye Place, London SW10 9PG

© Limbo Books Ltd, George Moule and
Steven Appleby 1984

ISBN 0 330 28489 4

Printed and bound in Great Britain by
Cox & Wyman Ltd, Reading.

Thanks to Nicky Hodge/Limbo Books, Nicholas
Openshaw, Anita Plank and Assorted iMaGes.

Contents

CREATING A LIVING KITCHEN   9

*Watchwords/Furnishing/Kitchen Things/Colours/More
Equipment*

PREPARATION AND DECORATION   27

*Become Your Own Best Butcher/Roots And Greens/Fruitful
Thoughts/Cooking To Camouflage/Basic Beautifying
Prettiness With Economy/Meals With A Message/Festivity
Fun/Heraldic Favours*

RECIPES   53

*A Glimpse Through The Mists Of History/Fare Of Our
Forefathers/ Food Like Food U Buy/Complementary
Courses/Cosmopolitan Cuisine/Food For Health*

FLUIDS   73

*Wine/Choosing A Wine/Storage/Serving/More Fluids/Cooking
With Wine/ Cocktails*

ENTERTAINMENT   95

*Who To Invite/How To Invite/How To Reply/Table
Etiquette and Decor/Eat In Like U Eat Out/Difficult Guests
Getting Rid Of Guests/When The Guests Have Gone
Entertainment For The Kiddies/Cooking For Kiddies*

GLOSSARY OF TERMS   125

Creating A Living Kitchen

1

Let us change your mind about cookery.
Try not to think of cooking as something to waste time until you open a tin. A dish should be a work of art — flawless perfection ready to be exhibited to the world. But, be honest with yourself, would your toad-in-the-hole stand up to the Elgin Marbles, or could your stuffed peppers sit in the same frame as The Laughing Cavalier?

Do not be intimidated by raw things. Many ingredients like to appear impossible to cook so that they can spend a few more days in the cupboard with their friends. Be strong — drag them out, tear off their skins and slice them up. Let them know who is in charge — remember, food should be lively but submissive. A lemon soufflé must be frisky yet obedient.

In this book are all the tips you will need to make dishes that are witty and charming every time you set them on the table. But, of course, to prepare lively food you must first create a living kitchen. Take a good look at the room in which you prepare your food — does it seethe with all kinds of unimaginable activity or is it a sterile fortress of hygiene and industry? A few quick improvements are all that are needed to transform even the most slatternly of kitchens. Out with that old boiler-heater! Tear up that rotting linoleum! Rip off that frowsy lampshade! Screw out that fusty fluorescent! Unblock that cluttered back passage! It makes you feel good just to think of it.

But let us dream for a moment. Look at our artist's suggestion which shows, in simple steps, how a kitchen can be rejuvenated.

1   *Homely, perhaps, but unforgivable. This man has wisely invested in a 'Darling' self-assembly kitchen.*

2   *It is widely available from a well-known home-care store and comes in a convenient pack containing almost everything you will need.*

3   You can easily assemble the units yourself, or with
    the help of that overnight guest, in a few short
    minutes.

4   A rasp and locking spar-wrench are essential (not
    included).

Watchwords

Here are some handy hints under helpful headings to aid you when restoring and using your kitchen.

Space
You should be able to turn round in your kitchen without snagging the flesh of your elbows or thighs. You can spot the owners of ill-designed kitchens by the jagged wounds that never heal.

Lighting
Good lighting is an inspiration and an illumination — even the humblest ingredients sparkle under smart spotlights. Outrageously expensive lighting is really a great economy if it is adjustable. Dazzle yourself and your guests. Ripen your vegetable retards under fluorescent strips.

Alternatively, turn the lighting down low and feed the one you love with all the tired old items you can't palm off onto anyone else. Romantic candlelit dinners mask many a culinary infraction.

15

Efficiency

You need not have a vast, spacious, hall-like room to create an efficiency-effective interior work area. You can still make good use of a tiny little cramped hole in the lean-to at the back.

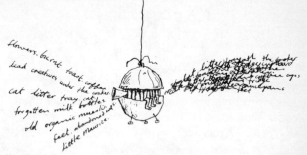

Ventilation

Nothing is worse than an odour, but cooking smells are a delight. Get a scent-segregator to split scents, odours, smells, wiffs, fumes and stale wind that drifts in. Alternatively, a good through draught will whisk away life's more unpleasant remainders.

Storage

The larger the larder, the longer they linger. In olden times the larder was a tiny room used to hide the lard from the rapacious barbarians.

Refrigeration

Food was first frozen during the ice age. Since the ice age lasted some time, early men and women found the preserved food extremely convenient. They could chip bits of mammoth and prehistoric vegetable, like broccoli or broad beans, fresh from the iceflow near their caves.

We have continued the tradition to this day, with up-to-the minute equipment recreating that far-off golden age of frozen food.

Use a *Minimorg* drawer freezer to isolate the corpses and dead creatures you are waiting to turn into spectacular dishes. The freezer can also be used as a convenient household threat, for example: 'Behave yourself my lad/lassie, or it's into the minimorg you go'. They'll keep quiet when they see the bad little rabbits and lambs come out good and dead.

Safety

Good and tough clothes are a must for the kitchen. More people are cruelly maimed as a result of minor scalds and cuts every six days than are mangled by vast industrial machinery. Remember – vinegar is a chemical cousin of hydrofluoric acid, and old friend olive oil is related to high-octane aircraft fuel. A few molecules rearranged can mean a dissolved limb.

Hygiene

Do not prepare fresh vegetables if there is still excess oil on your skin, as this is an ideal breeding ground for harmful bacteria. Gaping wounds can hide all manner of unpleasant biological items. Cover up cold sores, scabs, warts, carbuncles, and anything your guests might find unattractive. Perhaps a surgeon's face mask might help.

A little soap and water is all most of us need to keep medically spic and span, but if you are at all unsure, a heavy-duty industrial cleaner should be used to dissolve away the dirty skin cells, leaving the hands and face stripped soft and pink. Any portion of your body that has the remotest chance of coming into contact with anything edible should be thoroughly cleansed. Pop your hands into an astringent solution or rub with lemon juice to test for any tiny cuts and cracks.

Furnishing

Taxi Driver

Cobweb

Assembled   Collapsed ready for storage

The Bandy

Ronald Coleman

There is always space for a design conceit; perhaps that delightful but impractical chair. For a restricted area, our consultant suggests you choose a collapsible fold-away, or kwick-stacking type such as 'Cobweb', 'Ronald Coleman', 'Taxi Driver', or 'The Bandy'.

When choosing textile coverings, safety is absolutely the first priority, so fabrics should be flash retardant. It's also a good idea to find a unique fibre treatment which resists dirt and spills. With kiddies and kitties around make sure of a soil release finish; lighten your wash and be kind to that old front loader. Talking of mess, make sure your worktop always retains the cool, crisp look you bought it for. A trouble-free balsa wood or cork cutting board are elegant solutions. Alternatively, a natural veneer-style finish in melamine-look laminate is just the trick.

Kitchen Things

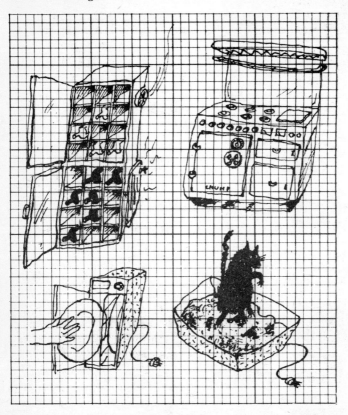

Let's make a little list of essential equipment: lockable cooker, keeps the kiddies out and the chickies in; spill-proof hob top; nice ice-cold fridge; *'Wineau'* cooler/heater; drawer-freezer; tables; chairs; base units; stainless wash-style sink; double dishwasher, with matching cat tray.

See our artist's projected grid plan.

Colours

Choosing the correct colours for your kitchen is most important, and some great chefs insist the kitchen is re-painted to match every new dish they create. Our consultant has selected this palette to blend with all natural hues and shades. The tints suggested will work together politely in any combination.

 Maroon Skylight

 Van Ghoul

 Dove Buff

 Meat Unguent

Bove Duff

 Maple Candy

 Blue Nippon

 Chameleon Yellow

 Ultra

 Hacking Orange

 Red Ripple

 Burnt Marine

Rouge Rippel

Brilliant Nut

 Greyseed Tan

 Pilaster White

More Equipment

The great chef Monsieur Snibbeau once said that *"la cuisine, c'est comme l'amour"*, the art of cooking is like the art of love — you don't need the right equipment but it does help.

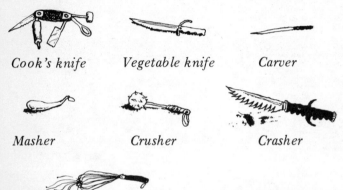

Cook's knife   *Vegetable knife*   *Carver*

Masher   *Crusher*   *Crasher*

All-purpose whisk for whipping a soufflé, fluffing up the cream, swishing away the bloated bluebottles, disciplining those naughty youngsters, or oldsters

   *Serrated finger bowls*

Gravy boat — the rigging adds that old world touch to a jovial picture pun to tickle your dinner companions

Mop   *Mup*   *Mip*

23

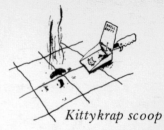
Kittykrap scoop

Fish-plates — with simulated shark skin surface to prevent slippery sea dwellers sliding off

Duck shears — for clipping the juicy legs off succulent ducklings

Steamer stack

Fish-shaped mould — the only mould allowed in your kitchen

Mouse trap

Sheep shears — flatten out those little lambkins and slice 'em in half. Change blades and trim off skeins of wool for garnish

Set of crinkled pastry cutters (see recipe for crinkled pastry)

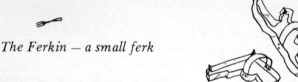

The Ferkin — a small ferk

Pastry shapes — make pretty
bickies for the kiddies

'Le Crapaud' — a popular French range of enamel wear
utensils inspired by the crispy flesh of young Gallic
amphibia.

Pompeiian butter dish —
with festive couple

Green glass cheese dome — to disguise unsightly spores
and growth

A covey of saucepans

Snake Mallet

Snack Mallet

Killer

Whether you have taken to heart these novel suggestions, and intend to totally rebuild your kitchen, or whether you have remained an armchair admirer, you are now ready to embark on the great voyage of discovery that we call 'cooking'. After all, it was a Cook who discovered New Zealand.

Preparation And Decoration

*Always light the grill as soon as you get in the house,
before you take off your hat.*

2

'Preparation, creation and decoration lead to elation'
(Bear in mind they may also lead to inflation, constipation and cremation).

Preparation and decoration are absolutely essential to distinguish the culinary experience from the mere meal. Think of a scrumptious dinner as a beautiful tree: the roots *(preparation)* sinuously twisting into the soil *(past experience and cook books)* support and feed the trunk *(the recipes and cooking, of course)* and the branches *(more cooking)* which support all the leaves and pretty bits *(decoration)* that makes the whole dinner beautiful. Finally the tree produces fruit, or acorns or conkers *(the food itself)*. You can have big trees *(nineteen course banquets)* or little trees *(snacks)* and all have their place in the forest of cookery.

Preparation

Get everything ready well in advance or complete
CHAOS will strike. Remember the tree: how can a
mighty oaken column of a trunk *(lots of cooking)*
survive on pathetic roots *(washing one glass and wiping
the carrots)?* Imagine yourself standing in the kitchen
just before that all-important cooked-to-impress feast.
The door chimes and suddenly you realise that nothing
is ready. You must face the silent ridicule of your
sophisticated guests, for lack of preparation has made
you a social outcast, you slut.

The very best thing you can do is to invent lots
of useful sayings to help you prepare, just like really
professional cooks do.

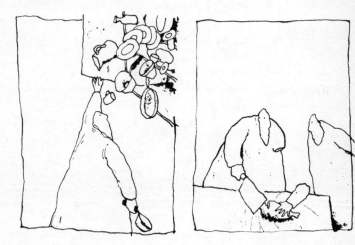

Store carefully   *Slice carefully*

Set carefully   *Stew carefully*

Before you begin cooking try preparing your
ingredients and utensils. Practise with a few lumps
of gristle or discarded sprouts. Substitute other everyday household objects for bits of food: soap for lard
and butter, red sand for sheep's blood, and paint for
other fluids. Pin copies of the recipe onto a docile friend
of the family or household pet. Slice ingredients
alphabetically *(Avocado, Bean, Cucumber, Demons-
bait . . .)* Cook ingredients alphabetically; you will
have to cheat a little as cooking times are precise
*1) Aylesbury Duck, 2) Bertatoes (mashed), 3) Cauli-
flower (that fits in), 4) Different Vegetables, 5) Everything else*

With any system one must be flexible. Slavish

obedience does not create a good cook. How many
dictatorships can boast a fine cuisine? Absolutely
none (unless you count Napoleon, but by Waterloo he
was eating poorly and his naturally sallow complexion
had become almost green. See page *83*).

Become Your Own Best Butcher

This little section is not for the faint-hearted.
If you like chewing on delicately charred morsels
of succulent flesh but refuse to pay the butcher's
exorbitant prices, strike out and become your own
best butcher. Buy a little hat and a stripey apron and
lots of sharp tools.

When any unwary animal nonchalantly waltzes
past, start thinking "how can I best divide this creature
into simple-to-sever segments?" Practise a little. Take
long walks mentally dissecting any animals you happen
to see.

DON'T be squeamish. Cooking is a brutal art. You
never consider the silent screams of tender turnips
untimely nipped from tearful taproots, so don't fool
around with baby animals. Earplugs in and cleavers out.
Leave hypocrisy at home.

DON'T be afraid to strike up a casual but affect-
ionate relationship with your prospective Sunday Joint.
Take pride in following it from gambolling quadruped
to swinging carcass. Imagine a poignant moment at a
dinner party when you turn to your neighbour and
announce, "I knew this chop".

Lambs (see fig. xi)

They are so skittish that there is nothing for it
but to rush in waving your trusty cleaver and cut them
up there and then. Try telling sheep to keep
young and beautiful if they want to be scoffed. Un-
fortunately many do not listen. They lose their looks
and taste and then no one wants to eat them. So grab
the mutton, tenderise it brutally and using a very, very
sharp chopper slice it into a stewing pot.

Calves And Other Bovinettes (see fig. xii)

These creatures are often so stupid you can cut
them up as they stand chewing the cud. Perhaps they
are resigned to their destiny. Perhaps they are taught to
accept their fate from an early age, who can tell?

*Rabbit And Other Fluffy Game Found In
Holes*

Choose your bunny. Take him/her on one side,
away from his/her friends and loved ones and ask
gently, "Have you ever considered a career in catering
supply, Bunny?" While Bunny considers a clever reply
stuff him/her in the toaster/oven.

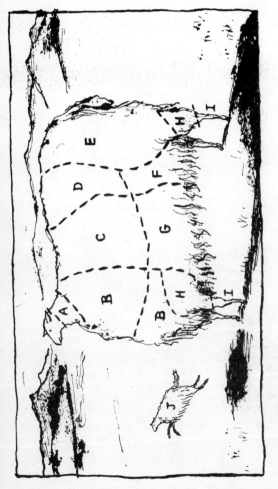

MUTTON (fig. xi)

A — Neck bit. B — Bust bit. C — Middle bit. D — Another middle bit. E is for End bit. F for Flank bit. G for Gut but. H for Hock bot. I — Leggies. J — Lambkin, how sweet.

BEEF (fig. xii)

Complex topography elegantly expressed. Parts X, Y and Z are around and about. Our careful artist has not forgotten them.

Chicken

This is a bit tricky, so follow the diagrammatic representations or you could come a cropper.

1. *Remove feathers by plucking (hopelessly slow and old-fashioned) or maybe use that old electric shaver (there is a use for everything in the flexible kitchen). Save those feathers for a clever garnish.*

2. *Seize legs and pull apart.*

3. *Thrust hand well inside.*

6. *Thrust.*

7. *Parry.*

4. Grasp knife firmly
   to joint bird.

5. Cut.

8. Cut, slash, chop, chop, disarm.

9. *Take hand, pull fingers apart. Human limbs are
convenienly oven-ready. Roast at Gas Mark 7 or
appropriate electrical temperature, dress and serve
to friends.*

Let us turn from fowl to fish. The little denizens of
the deep are quite well-made and easy to dismember.

Most Fish

Gut and clean.
Slide off skin.
Slip fillets swiftly from the comb of bones.
And if you believe it is this easy you deserve to choke
on all the tiny razor-sharp bones still left lurking
amongst the flesh.

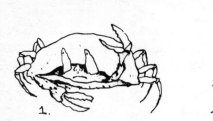 

Crab

Put on gauntlets. Plunge surprised crabby into fiercely
boiling water — careful of those nipper claws. Lay
protesting crab on its back — pay no attention to his
protests, he has no constitutional rights. Seize screaming
crustacean behind his nasty head, insert eager grasping
fingers between head and so-called fish and push body
away — his not yours. Stifle the creature's shrill moans
and watch its little eyes bulge on their stalks. If he
cannot tell you where any buried treasure is now he
never will, so you might as well cook him and eat him.
He has some poisonous bits so take them off.

   The principle is the same for dead crabs, but then you
cannot tell if they are fresh or not. Remember: *dead
crabs don't talk.*

Lobster

Evolution has disguised this crab as a large shrimp. It
claims to be more expensive too. Treat it like a crab.
For some reason the French call it a *hommard* but they
have a lot of different names for things.

Roots and Greens

Don't just peel them and boil them, use your imagination. Treat the vegetable as a friend of the family or an overnight guest. Try to understand what he or she would like. "Well Mr Parsnip do you fancy a quick steaming before lunch? Miss Cucumber*, would you prefer being slit end-to-end tonight or just my usual cack-handed slicing?" If you address your vegetables in this way you will be surprised how many people will find your dinner parties unusual.

*Contrary to most lewd imaginings the cucumber is generally a delicate female, an almost spinster-like vegetable.

Fruitful Thoughts

Rightly it has been said *"by their fruits ye shall know them"*. You can tell many things from the way those around you use these jewels of nature. An orange slung carelessly into a *crème caramel* shows insensitivity and intolerance. Whereas an elegantly sculptured kiwi fruit atop an expensive trifle conveys an artistic temperament with a barely-veiled tendency toward psychotic despair. The language of fruit is important to many great psychologists.

To avoid exposing your fears, desires and innermost thoughts you must use fruit in a new way. Try to think of a banana as a yellow cucumber or a pineapple as a spiney parsnip.

Decoration

And now we come to the little green leaves and
blossoms on our tree of cookery (see page 29). Just
think of all the sensual ways that food can beautify the
lives of yourself and your loved ones. A few deft
touches can make even the most bland and boring
dish lovely to look at, delightful to hold and heaven to
chew.

Remember: *decoration is the icing on the cake.*

Cooking to Camouflage

Decoration has a practical side. Careful camouflage can
make anybody swallow anything: *a little disguising
makes it appetising.* Colour, shape and texture are most
important in deceiving people. Try a few experiments.
Cut up boring and nasty food and shape it into dishes
you enjoy. Swedes can easily be made to look like
ice cream. Cabbage can be ground up and coloured
brown like a beefburger. Even the cheapest ingredients
can be transformed into something quite nice. The
kiddies will scoff up their greens if you mould them
into sweeties.

Just a few glacé cherries or a carefully-positioned
gherkin fan can create the shimmering illusion of taste.
Your guests will have almost finished your foul throw-
together platter before they realise the awful truth. You
have fooled them at last!

However evil-tasting your meal may be, the more
radiantly beautiful it is the quicker your guests will
wolf it down. Clever decoration can make even the most
timid guest a ravening monster with a bottomless gut.

Basic Beautifying

It is all very well to beautify your finest food, but what about everyday meals? Make an effort. Every meal should be a visual banquet, a feast for the eyes as well as the tongue, the insides of the mouth and the whole digestive system.

Lucky old supper gets all the fun, for high tea and dinner look their best, but what about poor old breakfast and your midday filler-up?

Breakfast

Rice crispies spell out the day's work. The boiled egg has been carefully varnished and polished. The toast is spread with hundreds and thousands. And a jokey touch: the coffee is served in a teapot. Even the milk and sugar have been brightly coloured. What a way to start the day!

And for lunch? Jazz up the old canteen-style meat and two veg. Look at this! Pink spuds, purple sprouts and orange ham slices, all with a happy-hat to laugh away the morning's blues.

(Colour these pictures. Mmmmn, we bet it looks as good as it tastes).

Prettiness With Economy

Once you have discovered the fun of food you will want to decorate every meal. But let your watchword be economy! Decoration can be awfully expensive.

Try to buy in bulk. Purchase hundreds and thousands in millions and billions. Also try liberally garnishing your edible offerings with those tiny metallic balls. They make mashed potato look lively and remind your guests to chew every mouthful properly.

Get a high-powered cream jet with fully-adjustable nozzle or a large pressurized canister full of industrial strength Jersey-style *"chrome"* (cream foam) for difficult-to-reach cakes. Our relations down under love it; they spray everything in the bush, beyond the black stump.

Try to reuse your decorations. Use sharp twigs and the leaves and fruit of semi-poisonous plants and shrubs to discourage your guests from devouring the decor. Food is jolly costly and time-consuming to prepare, especially these days. There was a Golden Age when tons of glacé cherries could be delivered to your kitchen by the grocer himself and all for a few shillings. But, alas, no more!

Meals With A Message

Scatter trinkets and gifts throughout your meals. What
are your guests' interests? Handyman? He gets screws
in the soup. Gardener? She gets tiny garden forks.
Fisherman? Little fish hooks. The authors of this book
were given a special banquet by close friends. Cakes
were decorated with metal type and diminutive quill
pens. Be original! Be creative!

How about a message in your pottage? Take your
advice from the fortune cookie. A slip of paper in-
scribed *"You decorate my heart"* placed in the boiled
vegetables has won the hand of many a fair soul. Heed
this old eastern poem:

> *Furnish your quilted rooms with desired ones.*
> *Conceal writings of lust in their eatables.*
> *Bring brandied broccoli blazing on a board into a*
> *bumper banquet bearing the legend,*
> *"Do not burn your delicate kissing tools".*
> *Your dove will become as a gazelle with lizards*
> *lips.*

(verses from 'The Song of Cinnamon')

48

Festivity Fun

Go a little crazy, decorate your friends with food and
your food with friends. Delight Grandpa with a garland of
brussel sprouts. Surprise your sister-in-law with her bust
in jelly. Edible portraits were very popular in the past,
and who knows how many great masterpieces were just
gobbled up. Rembrandt was forced to paint on canvas
to stop greedy burghers eating his work. His portraits
in icing sugar are sadly lost for ever.

*Knife (used for decorative and
amusing carving) and fork
(specially developed to hold even
the most mobile joint of meat).
Note the hygienic plastic handles.*

Heraldic Favours

After a few sips of tea and a sliver of buttery bread, the cakes and crumbly sweetmeats beckon. Atop the matt, smooth-as-glass icing sit the candles and the cake decorations. Originally, cakes were decorated to show their place on the groaning banquet tables of yore.

In the smokey chambers of medieval monarchs, *Baron Beef* and *Sir Loin* lounged in hefty platters. Pullets, capons, bustards, paycocks — all manner of fowl flesh graced the trenchers. The cry went up "My lord, forsooth, the sweetmeats misseth, save the mark!" So small heraldic motifs were placed on cakes to show their allegiance and favour; later, flags and banners and today, charming ornaments. Candles were first used to illuminate the midnight feasts of various holy orders in Burgundy.

Colour and assemble the delightful food decorations printed here. Simply give the kiddies sharp scissors, paints and lots of glue, then tell them to cut around the edges, fold the dotted lines, and so on. Charming and easy to make.

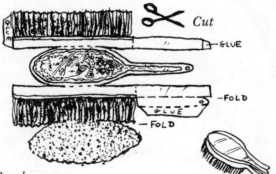

Hair Brush

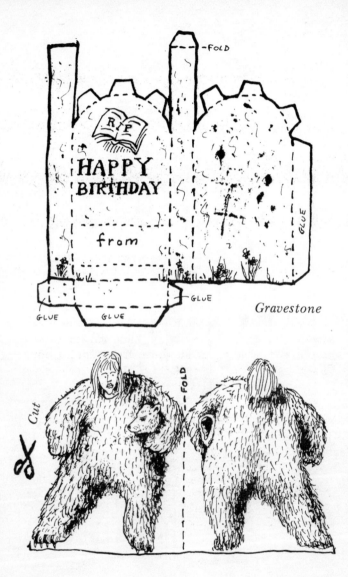

Gravestone

Bear Lady

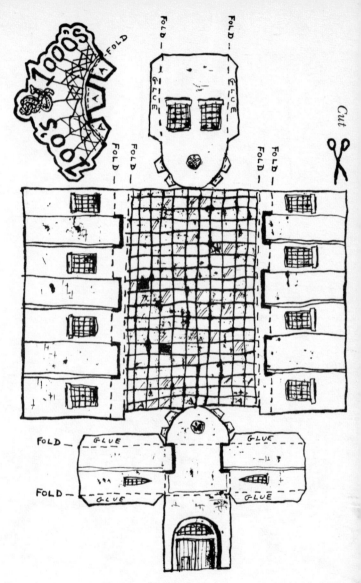

Hundreds and Thousands Factory

Recipes

3

Whether you wish to make the best of British dishes or food from foreign parts you will have to read recipes. *"Recipe"* is from the Latin word *"recipere"* meaning *"take"*. Romans and monks and the sort of person that spoke a lot of Latin, which was an early form of language, would write *"recipe tria ova"* [1] in a cookery scroll. As books became more popular and people began to speak modern languages they forgot the original meaning of *"recipe"*.

Today *"recipe"* means what it says. A recipe is a list of things and a method of putting them together to make something to eat or drink. How many other cookery books tell you these basic facts?

A Glimpse Through The Mists Of History

In the beginning, at the Dawn of Time, a flaming sun cast its rays across the caveman's breakfast. Solar heat lightly warmed his gristly lump of raw mammoth [2] meat. It tasted good. The cavewoman, who had been looking for new ways of preparing raw mammoth, tried dropping a steak down a nearby volcano. Then the cave-people tried vegetables, ears of corn, the flesh of other

---

1. *"Take three eggs"*
2. Mammoth, a woolly elephant. Imagine a huge lamb with a trunk.

animals, pieces of bread, and so the art of cookery was born.

Nowadays it is helpful to think of history as the menu of a vast meal with each age a different course. The Egyptians and the Israelites as the hors d'oeuvres, the Greeks and Romans as the starters (like melon), the Dark Ages as soup (a bad time for cookery when King Alfred of Wessex burned cakes), the Middle Ages as the fish course (banquets had many more courses in the past), the 16th, 17th and 18th centuries as the main course, and so on. But where are we today? Are we the coffee, the liqueurs and the mints before the world comes to an end? Let us hope we are just dessert, or pudding if you prefer.

Fare Of Our Forefathers

We can learn a lot from our forefathers. Let us take a look at two recipes from early in the main course, the Elizabethans. Notice the unufual fpelling.

The Arte of Preferuing, Jamming, Candying &c.

Ffruit Conferve
Firft flice faid ffruits.
Foak fkins and ftones fecondly in fyrup.
Helpful hint: ftand ffruit for four furfdays is Beft Way.
Caft fyrup off and ftraine in farcenet or fine lawne.
Fet over fire in Elifabethan faucepan * filled haf full wif fugar.
Fboil until ftiffe.
Fet for to ftand.
Put in gally pots.

Conferue of Damfons (anofer refipy)

Take bottle of damfons, prickle damfons, puttle backle in pottle.
Add wattle and fuggarl. Boigle briefle.
Waitle 'ater, Eat 'er.

They were lufty eaters in those bygone days. There are fables of tables groaning under eatables and potables.

*Fubfiftute fteel faucepan if preferred.

Fketch of vaft firkin quaffed wif gufto by Lord Effingham, fafhioned by our artift, Ftefen.

Food Like Food U Buy

Many of us are just waiting for our family and loved ones to say "This is quite good. Did you get it in a shop?" Never disappoint them. Always say it was bought and smile cunningly to yourself as they tuck in.

Fast Food

Food is a real pleasure but for many busy business folk, eating is a colossal waste of time. It is nice to know that sometimes you can buy something tepid and tasteless with only a touch of texture and just bolt it down. And so often with these hurried snacks you get double the pleasure. Most fast food has been designed to reappear at regular intervals after it has been eaten, recreating the subtle flavours of the original meal — culinary déjà vu. Making fast food in the quiet convenience of your own kitchen can be great fun, especially for the kiddies, they love it!

FISH 'N' CHIPS — a favourite of olden times

Ingredients:
Cod fillet, hillock fish, slink flounder, sand eel.
Potatoes — plenty of healthy shoots and beady little
eyes.
Batter — always best bulk bought in quantities no less
than 30 imp. gallons.

Method:
Heat oil to well past boiling point or until black smoke
forms thick pall near ceiling. Chunk cut potatoes with
cleaver. Dip fish and potato slices in batter and fry
until limp.

Serving suggestion:
Lift directly onto cheap newspaper, which should
contain articles with cheap and salacious details of
intimate behaviour. Allow oil to soak well into printing
ink. Place in overcoat pocket. Trudge round kitchen
until fish has cooled. Eat direct from newspaper.

Place condiments in used returnable lemonade
bottles. Pierce caps with old fork and leave half
unscrewed.

FRIED CHICKEN — a Southern Yankee treat.

Prepare as for fish and chips. Sever chicken with open band saw into four unequal parts. Ideally the chicken should be cold and slimey to the touch while retaining a searing heat inside. Mind those kiddies' little tongues!

PIZZA

It may look like a thick Italian pancake and a serious road accident, but it is actually delicious and so easy to make. Simply mix up thick Italian pancake batter, bake, and top with brutally pulverised tomatoes. Sprinkle with nuts, blistering hot peppers, rubbery salami (thick sausage with gristly bits), olive oil and, of course, parmesan (old Italian cheddar) or Romano (old Roman cheddar).
Serve in badly made cardboard box.

HAMBURGER — the best from the West

Ingredients:
Bulk buy soft 'bap' style buns or sponge trifle cakes,
ground meat (passed fit for human consumption),
salad stuffs, pickles and relishes (made from turnip and
vinegar and recoloured), processed cheese slices.
(Makes 14 million billion every week).

Method:
Dry cheese slice and pre-melt. Place salad stuffs in oven
and allow to wilt. Soak bun in ½ inch (1cm) cold water.
Force meat into patty shape, spray with oil and allow
edges to curl sharply upwards. Place between bap halves,
slap on everything else, press bun firmly and serve
upside down in pre-chilled polystyrene container.

Party suggestion:
For a special kiddies' occasion, dress up as a transvestite
clown in an orange wig. They'll love your charm and
charisma.

Complementary Courses

The secret of preparing a marvellous menu is to choose
dishes that complement one another. A Scots wifie
sought inspiration from the dour skies of her native
land and produced a perfect platter; haddock fillets,
mashed potatoes and butter beans, all boiled to within
an inch of their lives in a pressure cooker. A fine feastie
of pastel greys for her bairns. Try another favourite
from north of the Border — *Chicken Wee Maryland* and
an accompanying sweet dish.

CHICKEN WEE MARYLAND
(Its small size makes it perfect for a twosome)

Ingredients:
1 chicken (wee)
1 tin condensed milk
7½ oz flour
Dripping
Salt and pepper (optional)

Method:
Melt dripping. Fry chicken on high heat — only the pretentious undercook, and carbon is part of a well-balanced diet. Dust with flour taking care to use all 7½ oz and when almost ready to serve, douse liberally with condensed milk and return to high heat. For a charming touch, garnish with gherkin fans. Serve piping hot with wine. Remember: *even the most intimate moments need a little lubrication.*

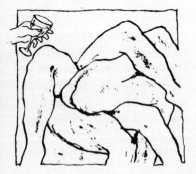

VODKABABS *(Vodkababas on a stick)*

Ingredients:
½ bot. vod.
1 pack trifle sponges
1 punnet fresh glacé cherries (red, or green if unripe)
1 tin of maple syrup or mollasses
Icing sugar

Method:
Soak sponges overnight in vodka and syrup. Drain on
wine rack over bowl. Serve the juices for a delicious
after dinner treat or enjoy them as you cook — not
too much now. Deep-fry sponges for 45 mins or until a
deep golden brown. Drain on wine rack again. Wine
racks are very useful. To serve, spear with cherries onto
knitting needles (these make handy chopsticks too)
and dust with icing sugar. Dip into maple syrup and
serve piping hot.

Both these dishes are also perfect for a romantic
tryst. But remember do NOT allow that special one to
follow you into the kitchen between courses. A rash
moment of casual intimacy could result in a dangerous
scalding.

Try to remember to digest well before any loving
words, as wind can so easily spoil a budding
relationship. The way to the heart is through the
stomach so keep the bicarb by the bed.

Cosmopolitan Cuisine

Cooking is an international language. We can all enjoy a *Paella Tandoori a l'Italienne* as an exciting way to get rid of foreign remains and an appropriate method of cultural combination. Yet it is to France that we look for a variety of classic cooking, *Cordon Bleu, Cuisine Paysanne, Cuisine Mincer* (delicious ways of cooking with mince), *Cuisine Gastronome,* the list is as long as the French can make it. Here is a recipe from *Cuisine Mincer,* to make you thin enough to mince.

Ingredients:
Vegetables of the exquisite nature to bring forth the nostalgia of summer days.

Method:
Finely chop the onions. Sauté with all gentleness in a
charming roux flavoured with charms of the juniper
berry (gin). The onions they remind you of the love
affair with the young person; first the onion she grows,
then you pick her, you wash and remove the onion
skin dress, when you have prepared her on the heat of
the flame of love, she make you cry. Discard the
onion, she is fickle. Try the garlic she is small and

cheap. Take the garlic, crush her to your bosom, she
loves the forceful treatment. Put her to bed with the
fresh young vegetable to confide her pungency and
experience of life. *DO NOT OVERCOOK*. The overcook he is like the jealous husband, he ruin the charm
of tasting and fleeting moments of passion. Take the
dish divine and press her to the lips and teeth, feel your
mouth burn with the desire. And the eating? It is the
transport of mutual heights of needing, wanting,
possessing and release. Have the good cigarette after-
wards. Thank you for the attentions.

Food For Health

It is essential to eat well for the good of the physical
system of the human body — you should think of your
body as a finely-tuned machine. Here are some
recommendations which you should adopt if you want
to stay healthy.

Vegetarian Grub

There is no need to eat meat at all with healthful,
wholesome fare like *Nut Cutlet, Cabbage Patti,
Coconut Steak* and *Tofu Chops.* Salads are good too.
Why pay exorbitant prices to eat raw vegetables in
restaurants, when you can eat them at home for almost
the same price? Vegetarian food need not be boring
but everyone feels much better if it is. Food is not fun,
it has a serious nutritional value and don't forget it. Let
your body know you are doing it the world of good,
gobble down that parsnip crumble made with whole-
wheat pastry that hits your stomach like a ball of lead.

"He that doth eate often lyveth a beestly lyfe".
Dr Anthony Boorde, 17th century physician.

Food is the great temptation of the flesh, but too much
flesh is no temptation at all.

Glance down at your belly. Does it hang pendulous
over your belt? Are great lines of flesh pinched
in by the straining seams of clothing? Do lumps of
pocked flab shimmer on your torso and thighs? Make
an effort — no one likes a big fat fatty.

There is nothing for it, you will have to diet.
Give up delicacies. Do not look at recipes for cream
sponge (see page 164). Do not eat butter or sugar and
give up absolutely all forms of alcohol.

Follow this diet prepared by our dietary consultant. Notice how a varied diet can be created with
only a few ingredients.

1st Day

7.45 Breakfast:	Lettuce, black coffee (no sugar), All-bran and prune juice (no sugar or milk).
1.00 Lunch:	Slim-bix and cottage cheese, black tea (no milk or sugar).
6.30 High Tea:	Lettuce, radish soup, grapefruit (no sugar).

2nd Day

7.45 Breakfast:	Glass of water (no sugar), lettuce, grapefruit (no sugar).
1.00 Lunch:	Slim-bix and cottage cheese.
6.30 High Tea:	Black coffee (no lettuce).

3rd Day

8.00 Breakfast:	Black lettuce (keep in fridge).
1.15 Lunch:	Black-bix (no sugar), lettuce cheese.
7.05 High Tea:	Grape tea (no sugar), black fruit, cottage.

4th Day

8.16 Breakfast:	Brick bran, prune tea (no lettuce).
1.04 Lunch:	Bran brick, lettage, tea fruit (no sugar).
4.00 Breakdown:	Ican'tstanditanymore.Givemea bloodychocolatecakeNOWanda threecoursebumperfunDINNER withayardofale.

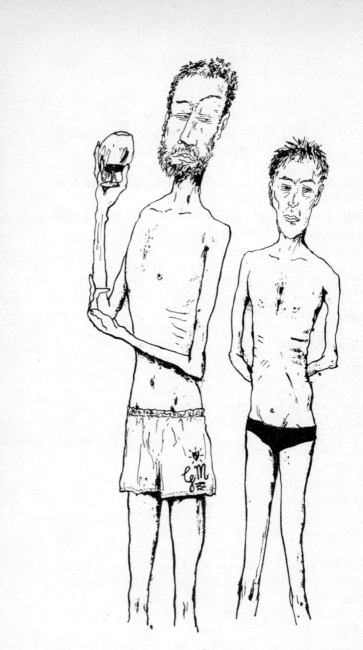

Of course, moderation is our guide in all things. Slimming means thinning, but some people go too far.

Thinnies are no better than fatties and no one likes a bag of bones. Unsightly knobs stick out of thin people. The authors of this book are much too thin for their own good — but for a few stone they could have got a real job.

Spend a little time and money on becoming just right, not too corpulent and not too scrawny. Your size and physical appearance will lead to success in your career and social life. Keep an eye on the magazines and change your body with the fashions. Alternatively live in a dark room for several years and only come out when your size and shape are in style.

Invalid Food

Slack service has no place on the table and it certainly has no place in bed. Invalid food needs as much care as the invalid. Dr Chef and Nurse Cook should buckle down. The ill demand coddling and cossetting. Tasty titbits and bland slip-down-easy snacks should be prescribed as required.

It is easy to forget the sick and serve them what we all eat regularly. In reality these suffering souls can choose from only a small range of food-stuffs, but the really creative cook thrives on restriction. The diseased organs and twisted limbs must be given every consideration. Put yourself in the bed of the afflicted infected, look into their eyes and ask yourself "If I were off colour like you, you poor thing, what would I really like?" Try serving things that help re-covery. Digestive biscuits and crushed nut lovelies break up into little crumbs and infest the bed. *Do not sweep them out;* they will work their way deep into the fleshy folds of skin, promoting shifting and turning that will work against bedsores.

A Menu For Increased Ease Of Movement

Prune compote, sennapod soup, curried banana surprise and apricot slipper. The invalid will be leaping out of bed in no time anxious to explore another room for quiet solace.

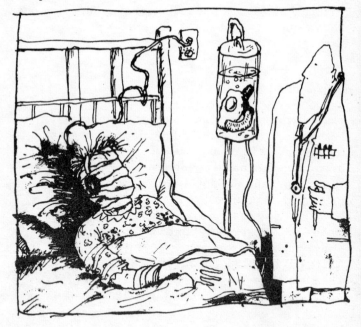

Fluids

4

Eighty per cent of our body bulk — sometimes even more — is made up of watery fluid. Four fifths of the surface of the globe is awash and life itself first reproduced in the primeval seas, only later slithering out onto the slimy foreshore.

Every glass of water we drink is simply teeming with life. Populations of tiny creatures live out their humble lives, grow up, fall in love, marry and die in every sip we take. Water is the ideal complement,

and compliment, to any meal. The greatest gourmet
and the most moronic, slovenly, lowly peasant can
enjoy a drink of H_2O. Without liquids we would all pass
on, but what passes through us as we pass through,
should not pass us by. Unlike the animals, who are
confined to water, we can choose what fluids we
imbibe. After water, which we all respect, whatever its
past, we must turn to the king of fluids and the fluid
of kings — wine.

Wine

Wine is one of the purest potions known to mankind.
Because of the alcohol contained in wine, few germs can
survive in it, and some doctors say that if you could
drink four gallons (18.1818 litres) of wine a day, you
would completely purge the body. You would also be
happy, carefree, oblivious of the world, all mortal cares
and pretty well everything else too. Many politicians
have enjoyed wine, and it has allowed them to make
decisions with minds unconcentrated and unclouded by
thought of any kind. This is the socially acceptable
face of alcoholism.

Through the ages wine has been the lifeblood of pleasure. Since the first dribblings of fermented grape liquid, crushed beneath the Neanderthal's foot, wine has been the passport to sophisticated oblivion. Even as this chapter is written, vinous ambrosia is being downed in fine translucent beakers, allowing the words to flow freely onto the page. In times gone by, wine has loosened tongues of kings, kinged the tongs of tuns, loosed the things of cons, and tupped the tins of loons. As the late, great, gracious Roman said — 'Nunc est bibendum'.*

* Horace, 37th Ode of first book, calling on Romans to celebrate the death of Cleopatra, an Egyptian filmstar.
Translation — 'Alright, let's get pissed'.

Choosing A Wine

Decide the colour and shade you want. Look carefully at the bottles. Some of the bottles are green to confuse you, but you can generally tell: red wines are darker than rosés, which are darker than white. The Portuguese produce *vinho verde* in a green bottle which could be any old colour. The label is your best guide. Has the label been attractively designed? Is there a nice picture on it?

Here are two examples to help you choose a wine by studying the label.

Château Lalique Rosechilled 1945 Mis en Bouteille au Château

Look at this boring label. Who would want to buy this wine? Is it white or red or fizzy? Where does it come from? In actual fact it is a red wine from quite a big area in France called Bordeaux. The grape growers there are very busy and produce lots of wines, so this bottle is fairly common and unremarkable.

Explanation
Château Lalique Rosechilled: This is a castle with two names. Probably *Lalique* and *Rosechilled* had to buy the château (pronounced as in *gâteau*) together, as they did not have enough money.

1945: A fairly old wine. It was found next to another bottle labelled 1961. Both bottles were covered in dust and cobwebs and had been put away in a dark part of the cellar *(wine hole)*. Obviously no one wanted them or the bottles would have been washed and dusted regularly, then stood up properly in the daylight.

Mis en Bouteille au Château: Bottled inside the castle. These grape growers cannot afford a decent modern bottling plant.

Conclusion: No effort has been put into designing an attractive label. Clearly the grape growers do not think this wine worth the effort. They are even too ashamed to send it somewhere to have it bottled under hygienic conditions. Drink it with fruit juice like Sangria (Spanish for *fruit cup*) or use it in salad dressing, or boil it up with some old scrag end of neck (see *Cuts of Lamb*) to make a stew. *Do not* give it to a family pet, as it may make the little thing ill — remember, he cannot read a label like you can, so he does not know what he is getting.

Price: Very high. This may seem surprising at first, but the grape growers are too embarassed to let the public drink it so they mark up the price to stop anyone buying wine like this. After all, they have their reputations to think of.

Snibbo Shippers Sweet Sparkling Red Wine

Explanation
Snibbo Shippers: A new company fast acquiring a reputation for supplying the freshest wines. In France wine is delivered to your doorstep, just as the milkman delivers milk every day in England. This has inspired Snibbo Shippers whose motto is: *'From grape to table as quick as we're able'*.
Sweet Sparkling Red Wine: A lively, frothy drink with a hint of crunch from the sugar.

Pic: What a lovely picture! Two girls enjoying some wine with a friend of the family in woolly trousers. Charming! Label design at its best.

No date: Must be extra fresh, see above.

Alcoholic content 60°: Pretty good, almost as strong as a weak whisky. After all, why else do we buy wine?

Produce of more than one country: Promotes international trade and co-operation. This wine contains grape juice from France, Italy, Germany, Luxembourg, Chile and one day, very soon, we may see American and Soviet wine in the self-same bottle; 'The best of all possible worlds' as Voltaire said.

Bottled here: Good, hygienic conditions. A swill of detergent in each bottle to keep it clean, and a bit of soap will do no one any adverse harm. If you cannot taste the quality of a wine through a few additives you are not fit to be called a connoisseur.

Contents: 60% fermented grape juice — a good percentage. Permitted flavourings, other flavourings — great care is taken to bring the wine up to a good standard of taste. Sugar, saccharin — the best of both worlds.

Colouring: Red they say and red they mean.

4 litres: Savour in bulk.

Conclusion: This wine should go with anything. Do not decant it — let your friends, neighbours and business colleagues see how much you care for them by keeping the bottle with its attractive label. The top is of a metal screw-on style and the bottle is fashioned in thick, strong, clear glass. Italian restaurant owners can buy this wine in bulk. It can come cocooned in plastic Chianti-style look-alike raffia.

Serve using an attractive wine cradle to impress your overnight guests.

Storage

Remember, wine is a living organism that needs great care. It starts life young, brutish, vulgar, ill-mannered — a regular little bastard — but given a few months matures to become tasteful, rich, well-educated and well-balanced. Only later does it become senile, right-wing and incredibly boring. Storage is all important to preserve the qualities which you bought it for. Shove it under the stairs or in some quiet, out-of-the-way spot, or stick it in the freezer (defrosting time: overnight or 2 hours in a pan of warm water).

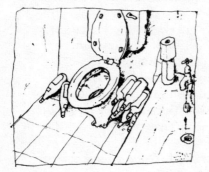

Serving

Wait until the last possible moment. Then the nearest gentleman should serve the ladies round about him, leaving himself until last. Forget equality girls, and take advantage of a time-honoured custom.

Bon Appetito Amigis!

More Fluids

Port: A red drink like wine from which the Portuguese get their name.

Sherry: Named after a girl. Bit like wine, made in Spain, Cyprus and other places. Known as a fortified wine, and originally drunk by Scots in the famous Fortified Rebellion; the Scots, unable to travel to London, confronted a large English police force after drinking at Hogmanay, on the Isle of Haggis, near Rum and Eigg.

Vermouth: A bit like wine. Made with a *bouquet garnis* (French for herb bag) swished about in it.

Framboise, Francoise, Kirsch, Kitsch, Quetsch, Aquavit and Aggravate: All forms of eau-de-vie, clear or white spirits. Often served in chilled glasses. Extremely alcoholic drinks made from fruit which enable the discriminating connoisseur to get pissed really quickly.

Gin: Dutch drink to give Dutch courage. Made from Juniper berries. Pronounced Jun.

Vodka: Russian gin made from potatoes and Colorado beetle.

Scotch Whisky: Made from malt, grain and other seeds. England is one of the southern counties of Scotland.

Irish Whiskey: Like *Scotch Whisky* but made differently in Ireland.

Bourbon Whiskey: American *Scotch Whisky.*

Wry Whisky: Made from the grain which makes Wry bread.

Rum: Pretend whisky made from sugar.

Brandy: Generally made from grape skins, husks, stems, pips, but tastes alright. Many countries produce brandies especially the more foreign areas. Napoleon Brandy is very dangerous and can make the drinker short, fat and green skinned with delusions of grandeur.

dolly   sherry   port   vodka   whisky   gin

Cocktails

Cocktails (kak-tal), probably from "cocked ale" (Eng. 16th cent.), ale or liquor that has been changed or "cocked up" or "cocked about with". The precise medical definition is "more alcohol than can be usefully ingested at one time disguised as something fashionable to drink".

In glittering movieland the cocktail is served ice-cold in a chilled glass with a spiked cherry or dainty olive. Crystal ice cubes from the capacious freezer chinking against the crystal glass accompany the babble of cheery cocktail banter. Almost everywhere else it is alright to serve a cocktail slightly tepid, in the wrong-shaped tumbler, with a bit of lemon rind called a twist. *THE CLASSICS* (Names, ingredients and symptoms — memorise these so that you can tell who needs a refill of what).

The Martini: Needs a chapter on its own. Use frozen gin, a murmur of vermouth and a virgin olive. Leads to

hoc   wine red/white   brandy

champagne   vulgar   shampain   liqueur

immediate clinical amnesia accounting for appalling
memory loss in politicians and prominent members
of the business community. Symptoms include "I
can't call the figures to mind at this time", "My party
made no such promise in its manifesto", "The cheque is
in the post".

Manhattan: Any quantity of bourbon *(American
Scotch)* and equal parts dry or sweet vermouth. Shake
with iced cubes and strain into a glass darkly. This is a
good one: there is an immediate sensation of charmed
well-being accompanied by paranoia of the sort ex-
perienced in New York City. How else do you think it
got its name?

Gin and Tonic: All the gin you can take with funny
fizzy water and lemon bits. Symptoms include high-
pitched horse-like laugh and a tendency towards
the sexless, landed aristocracy.

Gin and Bitter Lemon: Gin and a bit of lemon. High-
pitched laugh and a tendency towards anything of any
social class.

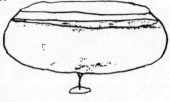

piss artist (sot)

Asbestos glasses for mulled wine and hot toddies have been banned.

Cocktail parties can be fun but check them out first. Use your discrimination: is the gathering you are about to enter a civilised, but sporty, group of wits at play? Or is it a bunch of drunken, bloated oafs on the verge of animal behaviour? Look for the tell-tale signs of

rented clothing, an excess of exposed flesh or unsightly
hair, indications of physical stress and inbreeding,
ill-fitting shoes or headgear.

Study these two illustrations and decide which
group you would best fit into.

Cooking with Wine

Many people are frightened of cooking with wine, but
here is Sr Senza Coglioni to demonstrate his delicious
burgundy soup. Sr Coglioni would never dream of
cooking without a glass or so of wine.

Yes, Wine is good.
And food is good.
Wine and food are good too
Gether they make a
delectiful combinoction.

Firstly we start to begin
First of all with the first thing
in the recipe: the ingredials.

Into the znoup go the first
ingredium the WINE.

First testi the WINE a litt bittle,
Mmm delittles!
Don't be afraid to try a liggle mord.
See? Good.
I cahn see at all now . . .

I cahn see at all now why
yew Engliss cook wittout WINE.
Where amai now?
Yes First try WINE. Mmm Good.

The cut into the znoup with
onewl and vegittles

Into the znoup oh dear
with the FINGERT
Nebber mine bit of meat inzere now.

Then into the pot we go with the . . .

Suddenly onto the floor we go

First try the WINE on the fl . . .

Notice how a professional like Sr Coglioni
keeps his knife especially sharp.

Ententertainment

Entertainment

5

The whole purpose of cooking, apart from an animal desire to fill the belly and gratify the senses, is to impress your guests. Why go to the heart-rending trouble of getting together the meal of a lifetime for the loved ones and companions you live with? Entertaining is the pinnacle of culinary endeavour. Seeing the looks of envy and jealousy on the faces of your guests makes all the hard work worthwhile. "How could those clumsy, stubby little hands have made that simply delicious *Potato and Aduki Bean Cobbler*" they ask each other. And you smile suavely to yourself and bless the day you bought/were given/inadvertantly borrowed this book.

It takes many years of hard-won experience to learn the science of entertaining, which is why most great hosts and hostesses are well on their way to the grave. Take a short cut to senility by browsing through the following chapter. Have a glass of good cheer at your elbow, a few cocktail sausages and put on a party face to get yourself in the right frame of mind to appreciate a wind of change. Remember: *entertainers are innovators.*

Who To Invite

Obviously those in your circle who love fabulous food will realise the trouble and expense you have gone to and will always want an invitation. But make sure you also invite those who *don't* like food and who *don't* understand the art of cooking because you can always tell them exactly how much it all cost and how long it took. One day they will thank you for this education.

Try to invite a group of like-minded friends and acquaintances who can keep up a constant background of witty and spirited banter. Add to this mixture a few embittered misfits who can enliven the party with

provocative actions or remarks. If this sort of person is not present the host or hostess must circulate with the wine, making the kind of comments that keep the party from getting bland: "It looks like your wife's breast-feeding the avocado dip in that dress", "It's a good thing I'm not a snob or the likes of you wouldn't be here", "Here you are Trixie. This gin's the nearest you'll ever get to a stiff one." Remarks of a sexual, religious or political nature are super-chatter fodder for any lively group.

How To Invite

A quick chat on the phone is not always enough. A little note, hand-penned or with raised printing, is the proper way. So few, oh so few, really know how to invite and to respond. The best advice one can give is to be truly sincere and accurate. You do not want guests to arrive in casual clothes, so say so: write *"informa but not sloppy"* on your invitation, or force them to go home and change. If it is to be simply a drinks party write *"Drinks and I mean DRINKS"*. Your guests will praise your invitations for telling them exactly what to expect.

How To Reply

Mr Snibbo knows that even if one has no desire to attend a function, one should always respond at once.

*Mr Snibbo has great
pleasure in accepting the
kind invitation . . .*

*Mr Snibbo would simply
adore to accept the
fabulous invitation . . .*

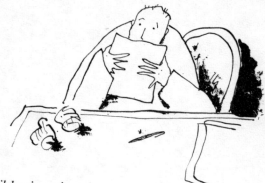

*Mr Snibbo is resigned
to accepting . . .*

*Mr Snibbo cannot think
of a suitable excuse to
decline . . .*

*Mr Snibbo has thankfully
just realised he cannot
accept . . .*

*Mr Snibbo has no earthly
intention of accepting . . .*

Mr Snibbo has vast delight in rejecting the
invitation of the two snobs who are too mean to
afford a decently engraved card to the nuptials or
wedding of the tawdry slut who cruelly jilted
said Snibbo and the rich old Bore whom she has at
last ensnared with promises of repulsive bliss on
Sunday 12th of October and I hope it rains.

Table Etiquette And Decor

Many people feel jaded by the endless round of simple buffets and stand-around piss ups. The dinner party is back in vogue. The table is the wheel that propels the dinner party and at its hub is the place setting. Here is a spectacular example.

The napkin/serviette has saved the crotch of many a well-loved garment from the careless slips of the lips and teeth — so why not learn to fold your napkins and serviettes into charming shapes?

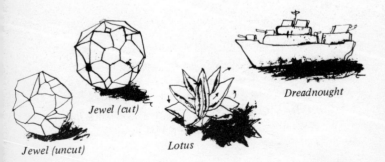

Jewel (cut)

Jewel (uncut)

Lotus

Dreadnought

If you are concerned that your guests cannot make the best use of your eating utensils, show them a rendering of this engraving, illustrating Simon the well brought up and Gordo the misguided. Simon is a nasty little prig but he is just the sort of guest to set an example. Gordo is very kind to his mother.

Eat In Like U Eat Out

The traditional dinner party is all very well and good but it is so predictable. Be inspired by the outside world. Recreate the atmosphere of a favourite, traditional eating place. Slip in a few recipes from our selection of 'Food Like Food U Buy'. How easy to transform an everyday evening into a never-to-be-forgotten soiree.

A London Pub Evening

Perhaps you have been to London on a trip, perhaps you have lived thereabouts, or maybe you have glimpsed its glittering nightlife on the silver screen. This is a recipe for an evening of capital English fun.

Arrange twenty people in a tight corner of your dining area. Ask them to shout to each other about football and drink warm beer tasting of soap. Serve anything difficult to cut up or digest while standing up.

Choose from a number of specialities found in most London pubs, including *'porpie'*, *'sosidge'*, *'toososidge'*, *'shepdspie'*, *'frenchpie'* (also known as *kitch Lorraine*) and the ever-popular *'plahmins lunch'*. We asked our cheerful landlord, Jack Sprogg, what the traditional components of the *'plahmins'* are called, and he answered in his colourful vernacular:

Ill-defined brown shining lump — *"Picklemate"*
Round evil-smelling, yellow globes — *"Pickledunions"*
Rock-hard processed dairy product — *"Scheeseinit"*
Thin brown crust — *"Sbreadinit"*
Starchy white tile — *"Udeaforwot"*
Hard log resembling French loaf — *"WosyorgameJon"*
These descriptions were followed by *"Effoff"* and *"Geddardevitt"*, his jolly way of saying 'bon appetit' to his customers, who are sent on their way replete (*"Ferwor I'm well full after that lot"*).

Our nutritional expert claims that it takes more nutrients to digest a pub lunch than there are present in the food provided. Follow the pub grub with at least five pints of beer in case an emetic or laxative is required: better safe and sorry.

DARN EH KEFF (Down At The Cafe) Evening

The British corner cafe: once it was the haunt of brickies and teddy boys, rockers and cheap little bank clerks; faded men and women who drank the same cup of tea for weeks on end. The true cafe died with the steam trains. Recreate the spirit in the convenience of your own dining room: wipe everything with diesel oil and beef dripping; serve all food out of large tins with mashed potatoes or chips; cover the first course with any brown liquid and the second course with any yellow liquid; drink tea from cups without saucers; drink warm lemonade or Iron Bru or Ginger Pop through straws that melt in the mouth; eat slices of day-old bread and butter without washing your hands. Serve liver, eggs and mushy peas, bangers, beans and treacle pudding, spaghetti, chips and mash — a pantheon of forgotten heroes that once fed the heart of an empire.

The Great Railway Evening

Remember how the excitement of a journey adds a strange spice to every bite? Does that "Will we ever get there intact?" feeling in the pit of the stomach really help digestion? Find out by recreating the age of the train in your living room.

Ask your guests to sit in long rows reading newspapers. Dress some as loud babies and drunken members of the armed forces. Arrange a long queue for the lavatory. For added atmosphere, cup hands over the mouth and cough to disguise the voice: "This is your chief steward speakin. The resterong car is now opin for the sale of late refreshmints, teacoffee, sindwaitches, alckoholic spirits, light ale and drinks, thenkewp".

Food: serve sandwiches made at least three days
in advance and wrapped in clingform-see-thru-stayfresh
wrap. Keep in a warm dry cabinet before serving. Filling
should include yellow plastic sheeting and pink plastic
sheeting. Serve also pie with pink filling in jelly, or
purple filling in jelly. Try to get everyone to drink a
paper cup of *teacoffee* traditionally served from a large
urn (*teacoffee* is thought to be made from stock cubes).

An Airborne Evening

Tie guests' chairs to ceiling with rope. Rock chairs
occasionally from side to side to simulate flying motion.
Serve all food on bendy plastic trays. Wrap everything
individually. Give each 'passenger' a one-ply napkin
(two-ply if first class), a razor edged spoon (dissolves in
coffee), a blunt brittle knife, three forks, an ugly wide
plastic glass and the stick everyone should use to stir their
coffee. Place deep, brown paper bags in front of each guest.
The host and hostess might wear fetching uniforms.

With practice, everyone can use airline food to predict
the weather and travel events of many kinds. Try it out
as a fun-filled party game on your guests:

*Coleslaw, greek potato salad (made with olive oil and
spring onion), minced beef goulash and parmesan:*
Means very bumpy flight, high probability of nausea in
passenger immediately behind, OR recycled food from
previous flight.

Veal or chicken: Made from identical animal, the milk-
fed chicken, developed by airlines in 1950's. Can mean
serious engine failure.

Fruit cup: Means violent shaking of port wing (with
cherries) starboard wing (without cherries).

Large chocolate cake: DO NOT turn your head. The
nearest child is covering your hand luggage with the
butter icing.

Brimming beaker of scalding chicory coffee mix:
Means air pockets immediately ahead.

No drinks: The radio officer and the captain are in-
toxicated and unconscious, but there is no cause for
alarm, as the stewardess, who has never piloted a plane,
is bringing this one down almost like they did in that
film seen earlier on the flight.

Free drinks: Means either   a) plane still on ground
                     or   b) plane unable to land

Free Spanish champagne: Your hotel reservations have
been cancelled and no alternative arrangements have
been made.

*Free food and drink and all the life jackets you can
carry:* Either unexpected forced landing or the airline
has gone out of business.

A Travel Tip

This is a useful ploy for simulation or reality.
For a peaceful flight, in a seat on your own away from
other passengers, follow this recipe. Take five valium.
Place coleslaw (see above) in brown paper bag. Lean
face well into bag and shout 'Ohmigod, ohmigod,
Gretchen, Gretchen, Rollo, HUGE" into bottom of bag.
Wait two minutes, or until attention of surrounding
passengers is assured, then eat contents of bag.

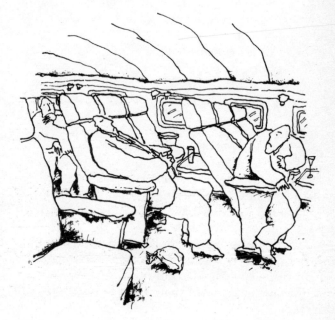

The Ferry Evening

The old cruise liners served food that no one could afford on land. Modern ferries serve a specially designed menu for those who must endure the constant motion of the briny wave, whether they like it or not.

Ask all the guests to stand on a sturdy table and persuade two hefty friends of the family to rock the table from side to side. Serve soft boiled eggs and liver floating in warm oil, fried tomatoes and pink link sausages. For drinks, *EITHER* warm pints of stout *OR* mugs of cold cocoa with lumps of butter floating near the surface.

Spray guests who get too near the edge of the table with salty water. Realism is important to true appreciation.

Difficult Guests

There is always someone who has had too much to drink.

1) Think of drunkenness as a compliment to your wine.
2) When he or she becomes aggressive, amorous, loud or political, *EITHER* stuff them with spongy foods to soak up the alcohol, *OR* find an appropriate moment and ask an old friend of the family to be sick on them.

Getting Rid Of Guests

Leave-taking can be the best part of the party. However it is always a delicate problem.

Seeing that people who are important to you take their leave:
Invite them to stay overnight. Smooth the linen and make them a lavender infusion. At breakfast on the fourth or fifth day ask them where they live. They will immediately understand that you value your privacy and will instantly go home with profuse apologies. Make sure you invite them again soon.

Making sure people who are NOT important to you get out:
As the evening drags to a close, cough slightly and ask them: "Does this house remind you of an hotel?"
"Is your watch slow?"
"Is the seat in your car uncomfortable?"
"Do you have a political objection to travelling so late on public transport?"

"Can you remember the Spanish phrase for 'I have overstayed my welcome'?"

Getting rid of guests who have no importance whatsoever:
Take them by the hand and say politely, but firmly "Fuck off, ball bag." *OR* imply that they frequently take part in a distasteful sexual practice which imparts a lingering odour that you do not wish to harbour in your household.

When The Guests Have Gone

The evening is over. Celebrate your triumph with a bottle of sparkling champagne. Open it carefully. Try twisting the neck a little.

Entertainment For The Kiddies

Don't leave out the little ones. They love a good party.
Try to mix education with entertainment. Make a
Road Safety cake with a realistic marzipan figure under
a favourite toy car or bus. How about an exciting
Action Man trifle with exploding topping? Or, for the
teenage kiddies, a Facts of Life cake, better they know
now than experiment later.

But the best entertainment for any child is making
real food of its very own.

Cooking For Kiddies

Cooking is great fun for the tiniest of tots. It keeps
them out of the bedroom and bathroom and confines
their injuries to burns, scalds, and electrocution.

Here is little Nicky with an easy-peasy, fun-
filled recipe for all you budding little chefs and
cheffettes. There is no sexism or role-playing in this
little kitchen: little boy kiddies *AND* little girl kiddies
must learn to cook. (Nicky chose her pink apron all
by herself, Granny only helped a bit).

Hallo. My nam is Nichola . I am 6 and $\frac{1}{4}$.

I am making a big surpris for
Mummy and Daddy in the kitchen.
Lovely PEPPERMIN CREMES. mmmm
mi friens like them a lot.

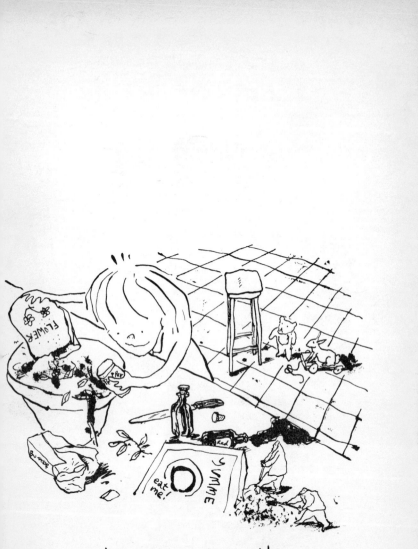

You can do cooking to. Here ar
the things. Mi frien s will clean
up the filty mess.

Mix up the flowr the sugar nice
green and red colour. Lots and lots
and the peppemin sense. I use
pepper and minty leaves for a
nice tast. mix mix mix.

Give some to a frien to tast

"Where the hell's Nicky?"

daddy says you har to eat thes
sweeties ver quickly or they get
to hard like elephants turds.
I like elephants.

119

"Your daughter's in the kitchen".

Cut the nice shapes — owl shaps for mummy and cars for daddy.

"She's your bloody child too".

Wrap them up nicely. Use Mummys silky scarve for a big bow.

Give th presens to Mummy and
daddy.

"Nicola, WHAT HAVE YOU BEEN DOING in the KITCHEN?"

"Well, the kitchen's fine. Perhaps she bought the bloody things. Who in God's name eats brown mint biscuits?"

save the mints fo your friens.

Glossary

A little collection of useful terms to help you through the maze of confusions that all the other cookery books try to create. Some of it is arranged almost alphabetically.

Cook   – to make food unraw.

Simmer   – boil madly for hours and turn off at the last minute.

Boil   – to roast in water.

Roast   – to dryboil or fry in the oven.

Sauté   – fry to charcoal on one side.

Cuisine Paysanne   – cooking for peasants. It is not worth it, they don't appreciate good food.

Cuisine Gourmande   – cooking from Gourmandy, a district of France. The Gourmands invaded England which is why we have French words.

Meringue   – fossilised egg white. A form of truffle. Old French saying: *"On est dingue si on n'aime pas les meringues"*. "Mad is he who reviles the white crispies".

Consumer   – a strange person who never buys the foods everyone else buys. This person is subsidised by food companies.

Consommé   – a French consumer OR a stupid way of describing a brown jelly. The word means consumed. Why would anyone call something "consumed" if it hadn't been?

Canapé   – something small one must eat at parties; be grateful it is not bigger.

Brunch   – cold lunch (American: *"Brrr! Lunch?"*).

Herbs   – weeds for cooking.

Bouquets garnis   – savoury teabags (containing all the herbs the herbman cannot sell).

Buffet   – disappointing cold meal with nowhere to sit down.

Spices   – powders, twigs, seeds, leaves, roots and other bits of dead plants they can't sell as herbs. Makes cooking taste different.

Chilli   – not chilly at all. Designed by Mexicans to catch the gringos.

Marinate   – to leave lying around in something wet.

Profiterolles   – choux pastry blobs that cost entirely too much. Less rolls = more profit.

Maggot   – why are you looking this up? Your kitchen is not fit to cook in – reread the first chapter.

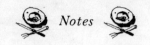 *Notes*